INSTANT ART
for
BIBLE
WORKSHEETS

Book Three

Compiled by
David Thatcher

Drawn by
Arthur Baker

Palm Tree

Acknowledgements

Special thanks to Rebecca Thatcher,
Heather Thompson and Anthony Stewart,
who all contributed some of the original
ideas.

First published 1990 in Great Britain by
PALM TREE PRESS
Rattlesden
Bury St Edmunds, Suffolk IP30 0SZ

ISBN 0 86208 130 0

© 1990 Palm Tree Press
  (See note about copyright in the Introduction.)

Cover and design by Arthur Baker
Typesetting by Typestylers, Ipswich, Suffolk
Printed in Great Britain by The Five Castles Press Limited, Ipswich

Introduction

The success of the first two books of *Instant Art for Bible Worksheets* suggests that they are meeting a need for this type of material. We are therefore delighted to be able to offer a third collection.

As in Books One and Two these worksheets are intended to be a resource for a variety of applications: family services, Sunday schools, mid-week clubs, holiday clubs and for use in day schools. They have been designed so that children of varying ages and abilities can use them at their own level.

The sheets have been born out of, and developed in, the regular family services of a local group of Christians in Rustington, West Sussex. Here there is one meeting each week where the whole family worships together — babies in prams through to grand-parents. Each meeting is flexible and open to the leading of the Holy Spirit, but there is a basic framework. A time of lively praise and worship is usually followed by teaching specifically aimed at the children: this might include pictures, a filmstrip or drama. Whilst the teaching is being developed further for the adults, the children are given a worksheet reinforcing the teaching. The children look forward to the worksheets, which have the added advantage of keeping them reasonably quiet! None of the adults needs to leave the group to look after the children.

This pattern has been found to be most successful, and we believe that many other groups of Christians might welcome the opportunity to use the worksheets which have developed from the Rustington experience. The sheets are intended to be used in conjunction with, and not in place of, an accompanying talk.

● day school use
The worksheets lend themselves to follow-up work from a school or class assembly or a class lesson, for which they can be adapted, if necessary.

For the infant age group, the word search puzzles could either be deleted altogether or replaced by a simple word exercise. For the junior age group, the picture could be replaced by comprehension questions, multi-choice answer questions or similar exercises.

● photocopy/cut out
Unlike some of the titles in the 'Instant Art' series, this book has been compiled as a collection of single page worksheets, the assumption being that users will reproduce a particular page (as a unit) in the quantities they require. However, individual items could be combined with other material and used in whatever way is most helpful. Our aim continues to be to provide material that is versatile and flexible in use.

As before, the pages have been printed on one side only to give the best possible quality of reproduction from a photocopier. The book's format allows it to be placed flat on the photocopier.

● Bible editions
We have used either the *New International Version* or the *Good News Bible*, the two editions which our research shows are the most commonly used by children.

● contents
A list of the worksheets contained in this collection, together with scriptural references and page numbers, is given overleaf.

● copyright
Material in this book is copyright-free provided that it is used for the purpose for which the book is intended. The usual copyright restrictions apply to any use for *commercial* purposes.

Users' Responses
Sales of books in the Palm Tree Press 'Instant Art' series continue to prove that they are meeting a need. The series is now developing in response to, and with the help of, people who have found material in the existing books useful. *Your* ideas or suggestions for new titles would be warmly received and carefully considered!

Contents

Find this story in Genesis 29

Then Jacob worked for Laban another seven years. Genesis 29:30

Put a ring round the right answer.
Jacob loved Rachel so much that he:

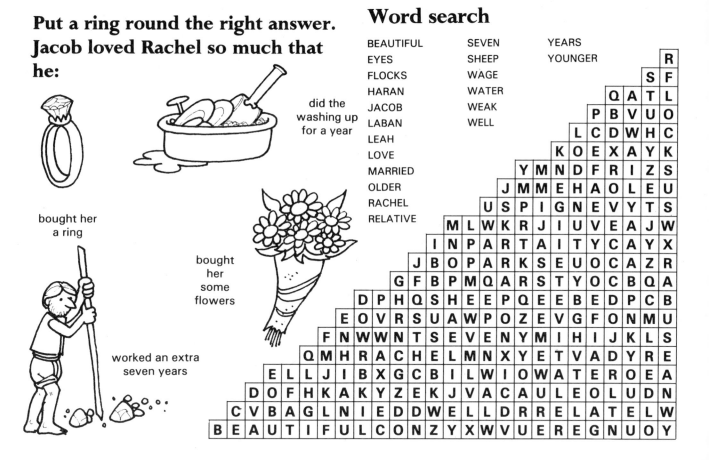

did the washing up for a year

bought her a ring

bought her some flowers

worked an extra seven years

Word search

BEAUTIFUL   SEVEN   YEARS
EYES   SHEEP   YOUNGER
FLOCKS   WAGE
HARAN   WATER
JACOB   WEAK
LABAN   WELL
LEAH
LOVE
MARRIED
OLDER
RACHEL
RELATIVE

```
                                          R
                                        S F
                                    Q A T L
                                  P B V U O
                                L C D W H C
                              K O E X A Y K
                          Y M N D F R I Z S
                        J M M E H A O L E U
                      U S P I G N E V Y T S
                  M L W K R J I U V E A J W
                I N P A R T A I T Y C A Y X
              J B O P A R K S E U O C A Z R
            G F B P M Q A R S T Y O C B Q A
          D P H Q S H E E P Q E E B E D P C B
          E O V R S U A W P O Z E V G F O N M U
          F N W W N T S E V E N Y M I H I J K L S
          Q M H R A C H E L M N X Y E T V A D Y R E
        E L L J I B X G C B I L W I O W A T E R O E A
        D O F H K A K Y Z E K J V A C A U L E O L U D N
        C V B A G L N I E D D W E L L D R R E L A T E L W
        B E A U T I F U L C O N Z Y X W V U E R E G N U O Y
```

Word search

BREAD
CAMP
DESERT
DEW
EAT
EVENING
FOOD
MANNA
MEAT
MORNING
MOSES
QUAILS

Q	S	O	L	O	O	M	Q	U	B
U	D	E	S	E	R	T	U	T	R
A	O	F	S	M	F	W	A	U	A
I	O	O	A	O	O	E	I	S	D
N	F	N	E	R	M	D	L	P	E
S	N	U	F	N	E	A	S	M	T
A	Q	U	A	I	B	R	E	A	D
T	G	N	I	N	E	V	E	C	O
U	M	O	S	G	N	I	G	N	I
M	O	R	S	E	S	O	R	N	O

Find this story in Exodus 16

Draw in here your favourite food.

What is it? Exodus 16:15

Put the first letter of each picture in the box to find out what they called the sweet white flaky stuff.

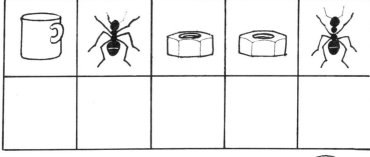

Find this story in Exodus 17

Jehovah-nissi
The Lord is my Banner. Exodus 17:15

Beware of lagging behind

The Amalekites killed the stragglers.
Deuteronomy 25:17-19

Satan prowls around like a lion.
1 Peter 5:8

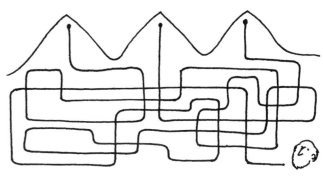

Which hill did Moses go up?

Word search

AARON
AMALEKITES
BANNER
HANDS
HUR
ISRAEL
JOSHUA
LAGGING
MOSES
STONE
SUNSET
WEARY

Y	R	A	E	W	B	A	C	Y	A
I	J	I	S	R	A	E	L	M	O
G	O	T	L	A	N	H	A	O	E
E	S	H	A	U	N	L	E	S	T
T	H	E	G	L	E	A	H	E	S
E	U	N	G	K	R	H	U	S	E
S	A	O	I	N	G	S	D	A	N
N	U	T	N	R	S	N	E	L	A
U	E	S	G	U	A	A	R	O	N
S	H	I	E	H	U	S	O	G	A

Read Exodus 26

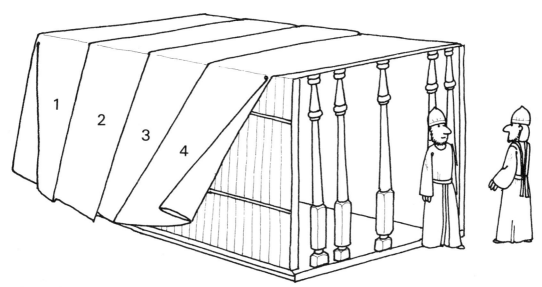

Using this code colour the tabernacle.
1 = Brown
2 = Red
3 = White
4 = Red, blue and purple

CAN YOU FIT THESE WORDS IN?

10 LETTERS
TABERNACLE

9 LETTERS
CRAFTSMEN
LAMPSTAND

8 LETTERS
CURTAINS

6 LETTERS
BRONZE
PURPLE
SILVER

5 LETTERS
SKINS

4 LETTERS
BLUE
GOLD

3 LETTERS
ARK
RED

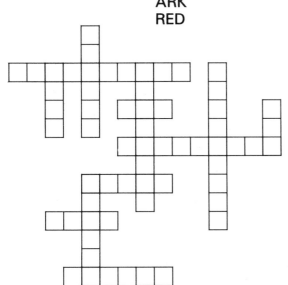

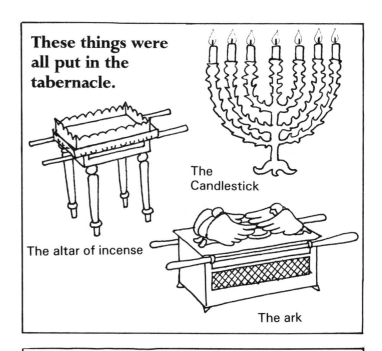

These things were all put in the tabernacle.

The Candlestick

The altar of incense

The ark

**To build a building you need instructions and plans.
Draw a plan of your bedroom.**

Find this story in Numbers 21

A B C

Which snake leads to the pole?

So the Son of Man must be lifted up.

John 3:14

Snake Facts

- Snakes don't have eyelids or legs.

- There are no snakes in New Zealand.

- Snakes can swim.

- Snakes shed their skins several times a year.

- No snakes eat plants.

- Only a very few snakes are poisonous.

- Only three kinds of snakes live in Britain:
  1. The grass snake
  2. The smooth snake
  3. The adder (or viper).

Can you fit these snakes into the boxes?

3 LETTERS
BOA

5 LETTERS
ADDER
COBRA
GRASS
KRAIT
MAMBA
VIPER

6 LETTERS
GARTER
PYTHON
RATTLE
SMOOTH

8 LETTERS
ANACONDA

How many snakes are there altogether on this worksheet?

Find this story in Numbers 22

Nothing is impossible with GOD. Luke 1:37

What could the donkey see that Balaam couldn't? An _ _ _ _ _ .

How many times did the donkey save Balaam? ☐

Word search

ANGEL   FAITH
BALAAM   KILL
BALAK   MOABITE
BEAT   SWORD
CURSE   THREE
DONKEY

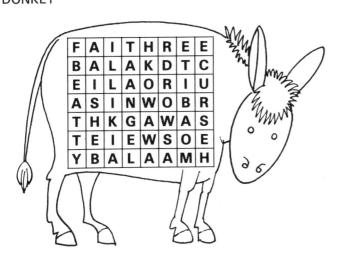

F	A	I	T	H	R	E	E
B	A	L	A	K	D	T	C
E	I	L	A	O	R	I	U
A	S	I	N	W	O	B	R
T	H	K	G	A	W	A	S
T	E	I	E	W	S	O	E
Y	B	A	L	A	A	M	H

Match up the animals with their sounds

Roar!
Squeek!
Baa!
Woof!
Miaow!
Squawk!
Talking!
Moo!

Don't forget — God can speak through anything — listen.

Find this story in Judges 6

The Midianite Invaders

An angel appears

The Lord is with you, mighty warrior.

Judges 6:12

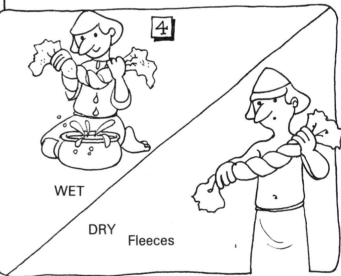

Cutting down the idols

WET

DRY　Fleeces

Words used in this story:

3 LETTERS
DEW
DRY
OAK
WET

5 LETTERS
ANGEL
BREAD
STAFF
WATER
WHEAT

4 LETTERS
BAAL
FIRE
LORD

6 LETTERS
FLEECE
GIDEON

9 LETTERS
WINEPRESS

10 LETTERS
ISRAELITES
MIDIANITES

Find this story in Judges 7

Gideon could have used these weapons . . .

But instead he used these

I am the Lord. Is there anything **NO** too hard for me? *Jeremiah 32:27*

A	◯	N	—
D	⊖	O	+
E	⊕	R	←
F	□	S	↑
G	⊡	T	↓
H	⊞	U	▽
I	⊟	W	▼
L	△	Y	▢
M	⧆		

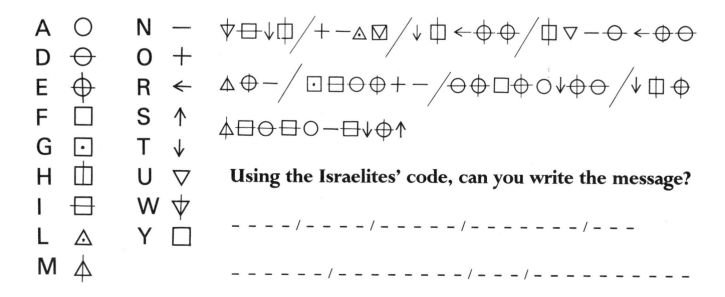

Using the Israelites' code, can you write the message?

_ _ _ _ _ / _ _ _ _ _ / _ _ _ _ _ _ / _ _ _ _ _ _ _ / _ _ _

_ _ _ _ _ _ _ / _ _ _ _ / _ _ _ / _ _ _ _ _

Word search

BARLEY
BETHLEHEM
BOAZ
CRYING
ELIMELECH
FOREIGN
HARVEST
LEAVE
MARAH
MARRIED
NAOMI
ORPAH
RELATIVE
RUTH
SAD
SISTER
THRESHING
WAIT
WIFE

T	H	R	E	S	T	I	N	G	R	B
H	O	E	F	G	B	H	F	I	E	L
R	M	O	A	L	A	O	M	T	L	H
E	T	S	E	V	R	A	H	I	A	A
S	A	R	V	E	L	L	E	L	T	S
H	N	O	I	L	E	A	V	E	I	R
I	O	G	O	H	Y	A	M	S	V	V
N	N	A	E	O	R	E	T	S	E	T
G	M	M	B	R	R	E	H	S	V	E
I	S	O	I	O	R	P	A	H	L	S
H	I	A	W	M	A	R	A	H	L	E
C	D	B	I	V	U	Z	O	S	A	D
E	A	W	F	T	E	S	R	A	L	E
L	E	F	H	T	I	N	A	O	M	I
E	H	W	I	L	E	R	P	L	O	R
M	E	F	W	S	I	T	H	R	E	R
I	T	I	A	W	A	I	S	T	E	A
L	F	H	F	E	H	T	S	P	O	M
E	L	I	S	T	G	N	I	Y	R	C

Wherever you go I will go.

Ruth 1:16

Find this story
in the Book of Ruth

Help Ruth get home by answering the questions correctly.

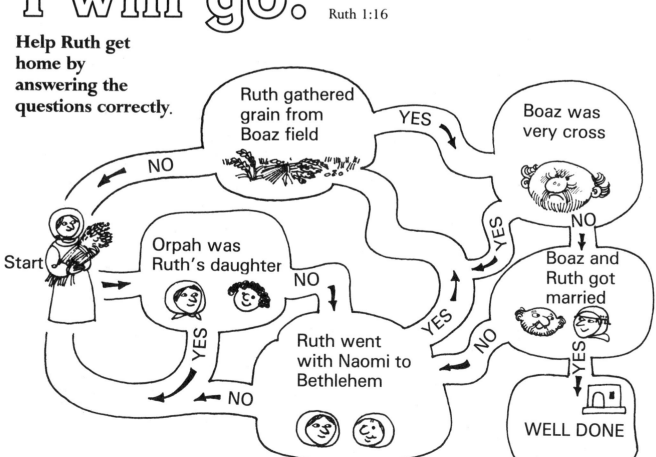

Start

Orpah was Ruth's daughter

Ruth gathered grain from Boaz field

YES

NO

Boaz was very cross

NO

Ruth went with Naomi to Bethlehem

YES

NO

Boaz and Ruth got married

YES

WELL DONE

Find this story in 1 Samuel 9 and 10

Which of these did the servant offer to Saul?

From the beginning God chose you.

2 Thessalonians 2:13

Help Kish find his donkeys:

Word search

S	C	H	A	N	G	E	D	N	F
E	G	A	G	G	A	B	O	L	G
N	T	H	A	N	K	I	N	G	O
T	N	O	H	L	T	Z	K	E	D
I	I	N	G	A	U	H	E	E	L
R	O	C	V	P	O	A	Y	R	B
I	N	L	E	U	M	A	S	A	F
P	A	I	D	E	W	E	N	E	R
S	E	R	V	A	N	T	J	O	N

ANOINT   RENEWED
BAGGAGE   SAMUEL
CHANGED   SALVATION
DONKEYS   SAUL
GOD   SERVANT
KING   SPIRIT

Find this story in 1 Samuel 24

Never take revenge.

Romans 12:19

Turn the other

_____

Matthew 5:39

Let him have your

_____
_____ as well

Matthew 5:40

Carry it _____ Kilometres

Matthew 5:41

Home 2 km

How many words can you make from these letters?

S F S
I E
G E O
E R V N

See if you can make one word using all the letters:

Join the correct words up:
What did Saul think of David?

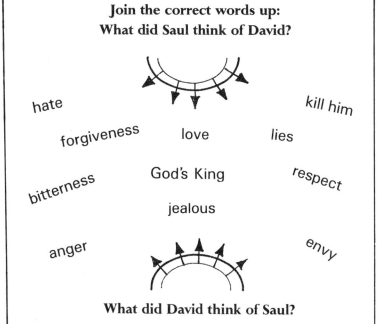

hate   kill him

forgiveness   love   lies

bitterness   God's King   respect

jealous

anger   envy

What did David think of Saul?

This story is found in 1 Samuel 25

In your anger do not sin.

Ephesians 4:26

Word search

B	E	N	I	W	S	W	O	R	S
I	G	Y	A	N	D	H	D	R	W
G	N	E	D	O	N	K	E	Y	O
A	E	K	E	D	I	V	A	D	R
I	V	A	A	N	A	B	A	L	D
L	E	E	N	N	I	N	E	A	S
A	R	I	T	G	K	E	V	B	W
B	E	S	A	I	R	D	E	I	N
R	E	I	H	C	I	Y	D	R	E
E	L	P	E	H	C	E	N	E	C
A	S	P	E	E	H	S	V	A	D

ABIGAIL DONKEY SHEEP
ANGRY NABAL SWORDS
BREAD RICH WINE
DAVID REVENGE

What do you get angry about?

People calling you names

Mum calling you when you are watching TV

Little sister spoils your picture

When you can't do your work

When people are cruel to others

When you get a flat tyre

Tick the correct box:

1. Nabal was a farmer who was: poor ☐ rich ☐ tall ☐

2. Nabal's men were: feeding pigs ☐ milking cows ☐ shearing sheep ☐

3. Abigail was Nabal's wife ☐ daughter ☐ servant ☐

4. Nabal was pleased ☐ refused ☐ to send supplies to David.

5. David became pleased ☐ angry ☐ sad ☐

6. Abigail set out to meet David on a donkey ☐ horse ☐ camel ☐

7. David was thankful ☐ annoyed ☐ upset ☐ that Abigail had stopped him.

The Lord is faithful to his promises. Psalm 145:13

Find this story in 2 Samuel 9

King David

David
promised to show

K _ _ _ _ _ _ _

to any of Saul's family

2 Samuel 9:3

Mephibosheth

Word search

T	A	K	B	L	E	M	S	F
C	R	I	P	P	L	E	D	A
S	A	N	K	U	M	P	E	M
K	A	D	A	E	K	H	D	E
I	M	S	F	A	M	I	L	Y
N	V	E	J	T	V	B	N	T
S	E	A	O	A	A	O	I	G
T	M	S	D	T	S	S	K	D
H	J	O	N	A	T	H	A	N
P	K	I	N	D	N	E	S	S
E	J	R	F	E	A	T	N	E
M	O	C	J	O	N	H	T	A

CRIPPLED
DAVID
EAT
FAMILY
FEET
JONATHAN
KINDNESS
KING
MEPHIBOSHETH
SAUL
SON
TABLE

Some of God's Promises. Join the verse to the promise:

1 John 2:25	No more flooding
Genesis 9:15	I will always be with you
Ephesians 1:13	I will forgive sins
1 John 1:9	Holy Spirit
Matthew 28:20	Eternal Life

Colour in the shapes with a dot:

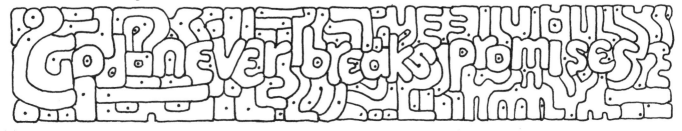

Find this story in 2 Samuel 11-12

We take every thought captive and make it obey Christ.

2 Corinthians 10:5

Word search

BATH   NATHAN   RICHMAN   WAR
BATHSHEBA   PALACE   ROOF   WIFE
DAVID   POORMAN   URIAH
LAMB

B	P	E	N	A	H	T	A	N	L	B	P
R	A	W	B	T	R	O	O	N	A	M	A
I	L	M	A	D	U	R	D	T	H	A	L
C	A	B	E	H	S	H	T	A	B	R	C
L	C	O	E	F	I	W	I	L	V	E	E
S	E	H	P	O	O	R	M	A	N	I	S
T	L	M	A	N	U	O	B	M	V	A	D
H	N	A	M	H	C	I	R	M	O	O	R

List any bad thoughts you have had trouble with:—

_____
_____
_____
_____

Now pray this prayer:
Dear Lord,
I'm sorry for thinking these wrong thoughts. Help me to think thoughts that please you,
Amen

RICHMAN

POORMAN

_ _ _ _ _ S H E B A

NABOTH

GRAPES VINEYARD

AHAB

PALACE

STONES

VEGETABLES GARDEN

JEZEBEL

LETTERS ELIJAH

Word search

A	D	G	P	A	L	A	C	E	J	M
V	E	G	E	T	A	B	L	E	S	S
I	E	D	G	J	M	P	E	U	T	V
N	Y	B	E	H	A	K	T	L	O	Q
E	L	I	J	A	H	S	T	N	N	Z
Y	C	F	E	I	A	L	E	Q	E	R
A	U	X	Z	A	B	D	R	G	S	J
R	M	P	E	S	V	Y	S	E	B	E
D	H	K	B	N	Q	H	P	W	Z	C
F	O	L	E	Q	N	A	B	O	T	H
R	U	A	L	D	R	G	J	F	R	S
V	Y	B	E	G	A	R	D	E	N	H

Don't do anything from selfish ambition.

Find this story in
1 Kings 21

Philippians 2:3

Unscramble these vegetables:

1. KELE _ _ _ _

2. RORACT _ _ _ _ _ _

3. TAPOOT _ _ _ _ _ _

4. HIARDS _ _ _ _ _ _

5. CUTETLE _ _ _ _ _ _ _

6. BECAGAB _ _ _ _ _ _ _

How many different vegetables can you see?

How many pots is the widow filling from her jug?

Find this story in 2 Kings 4

God richly provides us with everything we need.

1 Timothy 6:17

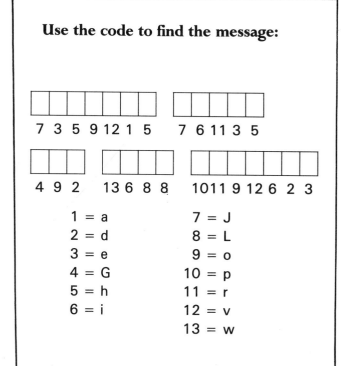

* See how many different words you can make from these letters.
* Can you make one word out of all of them?

Use the code to find the message:

7 3 5 9 12 1 5   7 6 11 3 5

4 9 2   13 6 8 8   10 11 9 12 6 2 3

1 = a	7 = J
2 = d	8 = L
3 = e	9 = o
4 = G	10 = p
5 = h	11 = r
6 = i	12 = v
	13 = w

Sennacherib,
King of Assyria,
fought against the
people of God.

Hezekiah,
King of Judah,
was a good king
in God's eyes.

This story is in 2 Kings 18

There is a time to be silent and a time to speak.

Ecclesiastes 3:7

Look at verse 4

HEZEKIAH TRUSTED IN
THE LORD, THE GOD OF
ISRAEL.

HE WAS FAITHFUL TO
THE LORD.

Word search

S	E	O	N	D	R	O	L	N	E	A
C	H	F	E	E	R	L	I	B	H	O
O	H	D	I	H	H	F	U	N	T	G
R	S	E	L	Z	A	T	L	D	E	I
D	L	I	Z	L	I	U	H	E	Z	E
S	O	R	D	E	F	L	G	O	D	K
I	R	B	R	H	K	O	T	H	A	I
R	D	U	T	F	E	I	F	W	O	T
A	F	I	L	H	E	A	A	E	T	W
E	A	L	T	D	I	N	S	H	T	E
F	D	E	T	S	U	R	T	I	S	N
L	U	F	H	G	O	E	L	R	E	W
O	L	E	A	R	S	I	H	F	A	U
W	G	O	N	O	L	D	E	S	U	L

This story is in 2 Kings 19

Leave all your worries with him, because he cares for you.

1 Peter 5:8

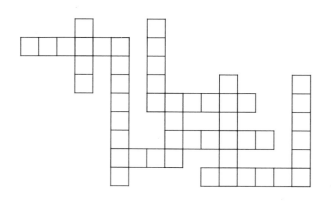

See if you can fit these words in.

4 LETTERS	6 LETTERS	8 LETTERS
ARMY	ISAIAH	HEZEKIAH
CITY	LETTER	
KING	PEOPLE	
	PRAYER	
5 LETTERS	SCARED	
WALLS	TEMPLE	

Do any of these worry you?

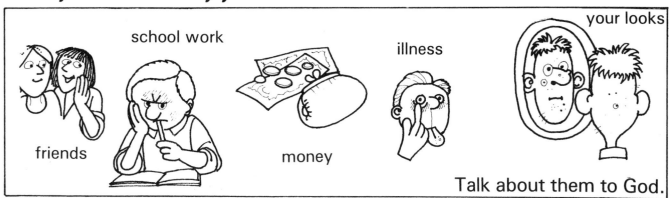

your looks

school work

illness

friends

money

Talk about them to God.

Word search

This story is in 2 Kings 20

A	S	D	U	L	N	H	R	V	P	G	H
B	E	L	I	G	O	E	U	S	G	I	F
E	I	O	I	U	C	Z	A	N	E	V	U
N	U	S	D	O	O	E	I	S	E	I	L
A	M	H	V	H	B	K	U	T	C	L	S
P	L	E	Z	A	P	I	S	A	I	A	H
E	R	Q	R	K	Y	A	H	I	T	G	A
H	G	O	O	D	Z	H	M	R	L	A	D
S	T	E	P	S	M	O	D	W	U	I	O
I	T	E	M	H	B	T	V	A	O	M	W
B	P	O	S	B	E	R	P	Y	P	N	E
D	I	E	U	N	A	T	E	M	P	L	E

BOIL PROPHET
DIE RECOVER
FIGS SHADOW
GOOD SIGN
HEZEKIAH STAIRWAY
ILL STEPS
ISAIAH SUN
KING TEMPLE
POULTICE TEN

I have heard your prayer.

2 Kings 20:5

To find how many extra years to his life Hezekiah was promised, write the first letter of each picture in each box.

Find this story in Nehemiah 1 and 2

Word search

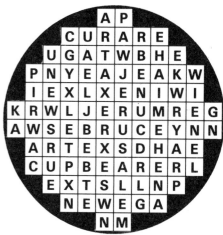

ARTAXERXES   NEWS
CUPBEARER   PRAYER
JERUSALEM   SAD
KING   WALLS
NEHEMIAH   WINE

Nehemiah prayed.

Fill in this verse : Matthew 7:7

A _ _
and you will receive
S _ _ _
and you will find
K _ _ _ _
and the door will be opened to you.

Find the ten differences between these two pictures.

Find this story in Nehemiah 3 to 6

Nehemiah kept going.

These men tried to stop Nehemiah.

Draw in their faces.

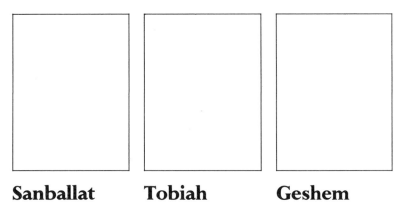

Sanballat   Tobiah   Geshem

GALATIANS 6:9

SO LET US NOT BECOME TIRED
OF DOING GOOD, FOR IF WE
DO NOT GIVE UP THE TIME WILL
COME WHEN WE WILL REAP THE HARVEST.

Word search

J	G	O	N	H	T	F	H	M	O	T	S	U
L	A	R	O	A	N	O	I	C	O	E	T	P
K	L	Y	E	R	L	R	N	N	A	V	C	H
L	A	I	C	V	H	D	J	L	S	I	J	L
O	T	F	W	E	M	R	Y	D	O	G	T	H
H	I	H	T	S	V	O	M	T	N	H	I	C
M	A	W	O	T	H	S	W	I	L	L	R	N
C	N	S	T	H	E	N	O	T	K	L	E	Y
E	S	D	E	O	R	D	O	H	T	Y	D	P
Q	U	M	D	O	G	A	W	E	L	A	I	T
I	O	A	N	S	V	E	H	R	S	E	T	H
C	X	Y	L	E	T	O	E	W	D	U	F	G
M	N	P	T	H	C	I	N	T	N	S	B	R
I	A	A	N	T	C	H	M	G	O	O	D	N
O	B	E	C	O	M	E	P	E	T	H	S	T
D	M	R	O	F	H	C	D	F	J	E	A	J
K	Y	N	O	H	W	E	H	V	A	I	S	T

Find all the words of this verse from the Bible.

Find this story in Nehemiah 8 to 10

Nehemiah promised.

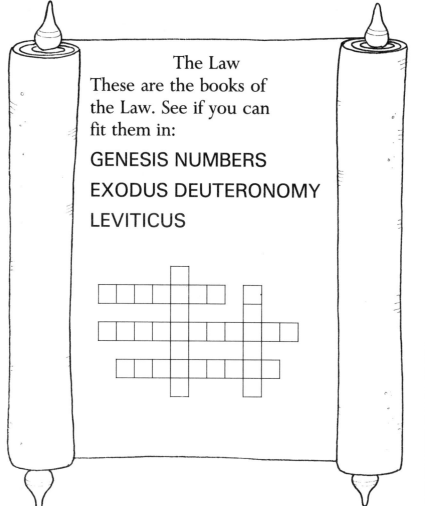

The Law
These are the books of
the Law. See if you can
fit them in:

GENESIS NUMBERS

EXODUS DEUTERONOMY

LEVITICUS

**Can you make at least
10 words from PROMISED?**

Word search

THE JOY OF THE LORD

IS YOUR STRENGTH.

Nehemiah 8:10

O	S	N	T	H	L	D	S	U	J	D	L	G
E	Y	T	E	O	Y	R	T	Y	R	U	O	Y
J	O	S	R	U	O	O	R	E	S	N	R	J
E	H	T	J	E	T	L	N	O	G	T	H	O
L	E	R	H	E	N	S	T	F	E	N	G	T
O	G	E	S	N	O	G	S	E	L	F	T	H
D	J	N	T	Y	S	R	T	N	I	S	L	E
E	D	O	R	S	T	H	O	H	E	T	E	S
L	O	G	Y	L	O	R	N	E	T	H	S	O

Find this story in Nehemiah 12

Nehemiah rejoiced.

Draw in happy faces:

Try and learn this verse:
Rejoice in the Lord always.
I will say it again: Rejoice!
Philippians 4:4

Word search

S	P	I	G	T	H	S	O	U	T
E	T	U	O	H	S	J	I	Y	E
L	M	G	L	A	D	N	E	S	S
C	P	N	S	N	Y	O	J	N	I
H	W	I	L	K	P	I	E	A	A
A	A	S	A	F	P	T	F	I	R
R	L	I	B	U	A	A	U	C	P
P	L	J	M	L	H	C	L	I	L
S	S	O	Y	E	R	I	T	S	M
H	E	L	C	N	H	D	C	U	P
R	E	J	O	I	C	E	T	M	U
E	L	S	H	G	L	D	N	E	N

CYMBALS   NEHEMIAH
DEDICATION   PRAISE
GLADNESS   REJOICE
HAPPY   SHOUT
HARPS   SING
JOY   THANKFUL
MUSICIANS   WALLS

Word search

CAMELS   SEVEN
CATTLE   SHEEP
DAUGHTERS   SONS
DONKEYS   THREE
JOB   UZ

	J	E	O	C				
	O	S	H	E	E	P		
B	T	N	Y	L	M	K	G	
I	E	L	T	T	A	C	V	O	U
T	D	S	Y	E	K	N	O	D	Z
N	D	A	U	G	H	T	E	R	S
I	C	A	M	E	L	S	H	E	V
L	S	N	O	S	K	V	G	
H	T	H	R	E	E			
D	W	N	E					

Three of
Job's friends

Eliphaz   Bildad

Zophar

Tick the correct box:

Job was   rich ☐   poor ☐
Job had   2 sons ☐   7 sons ☐
Job had   2 daughters ☐   3 daughters ☐
Job was   a good man ☐   a bad man ☐
Job was   married ☐   was not married ☐

Fit the jigsaw pieces into their places

come   tested   He   When   forth   shall

gold.   as   I   me   has

Job 23:10

1. Jeremiah dictates, Baruch writes. v4

Find this story in Jeremiah 36

2. Baruch reads to the people. v.10

3. Baruch goes to the officials. v.14

4. Baruch reads to the officials. v.16

5. The King cuts and burns the scroll. v.23

6. Jeremiah dictates again. Baruch writes again. v.32

All Scripture is inspired by God.

2 Timothy 3:16

Word search

Here are the first books of the Bible.

GENESIS
EXODUS
LEVITICUS
NUMBERS
DEUTERONOMY
JOSHUA
JUDGES
RUTH
SAMUEL
KINGS
CHRONICLES
EZRA
NEHEMIAH
ESTHER
JOB
PSALMS

E	X	O	S	R	S	M	L	A	S	P
D	M	Y	U	J	O	S	H	U	A	M
C	E	T	C	U	L	H	S	J	M	O
R	H	U	I	D	N	E	R	B	U	N
O	A	S	T	G	U	J	E	U	E	O
N	I	K	I	E	V	Z	B	V	L	R
I	M	I	V	S	R	I	M	O	Z	E
N	E	N	E	A	E	O	U	R	J	H
G	H	G	L	D	S	N	N	I	K	T
N	E	S	U	D	O	X	E	O	T	S
E	N	J	N	E	H	E	M	G	M	E
C	H	R	O	N	I	C	L	E	S	Y

Find this story in Jeremiah 38:1-13

Friends always show their love.

Proverbs 17:17

Word search

E	C	I	T	E	R	M	U	R	E
R	B	G	B	A	C	F	O	O	M
S	J	E	G	N	I	K	S	P	B
O	E	S	D	E	D	O	O	F	E
E	B	E	E	M	W	E	L	L	D
L	R	O	U	P	E	O	D	K	M
D	I	D	C	S	O	L	I	D	E
F	H	A	I	M	E	R	E	J	L
O	A	C	T	E	G	O	R	C	E
D	M	E	Y	T	I	C	S	E	H

CITY   MUD
EBEDMELECH   RAGS
FOOD   ROPE
JEREMIAH   SOLDIERS
KING   WELL

Put the first letter of each picture in the empty box below and find what word is made:

John said:

Jesus must become more important while I become less important.

John 3:30

Look at this carefully to work out what Zechariah said:

h	m	s
e	j	o
a	i	n

Word search

Find this story in Luke 1

T	E	M	P	L	S				
E	N	I	L	E	E	N	V		
A	L	A	O	G	N	H	E	I	E
S	N	P	B	N	I	O	N	L	S	L	J
O	G	M	A	A	J	S	M	U	D	E	O
L	U	E	P	R	B	U	I	Z	A	I	N
D	L	T	T	B	M	Y	E	V	T	R	O
L	E	L	I	Z	A	B	E	T	H	B	N
T	S	M	Z	E	C	H	A	R	I	A	H
T	S	E	I	R	P	G	S	T	G
T	E	V	P	R	I	E	S
B	S	A	V	E	J	G

ANGEL   JOHN
BABY   PRIEST
BAPTIZE   SON
DUMB   TEMPLE
ELIZABETH   VISION
GABRIEL   ZECHARIAH

When John was older he wore clothes of camels hair, and his food was locusts and wild honey.
He prepared the way for Jesus. **See Matthew 3: 1-4**

Later John was put in prison because King Herod didn't like what John was saying. On the King's birthday John was killed as a present for his daughter.
See Matthew 14:1-12

1 Happy are the poor in spirit, for the kingdom of heaven belongs to them.

2 Happy are those who mourn,

they will be comforted.

3 Happy are those who are humble, for they will inherit the earth.

4 Happy are those who hunger and thirst for righteousness, for they will be filled.

5 Happy are those who are merciful to others, for God will be merciful to them.

Happy are those who are persecuted, for theirs is the kingdom of heaven.

6 Happy are the pure in heart,

for they will see God.

7 Happy are the peacemakers,

for they will be called the sons of God.

8

Matthew 5:3-10

Word search

BEATITUDES	MERCIFUL
GOD	PEACEMAKERS
HAPPY	PERSECUTED
HEAVEN	POOR
HUMBLE	PURE
HUNGER	THIRST
KINGDOM	

The Beatitudes
or
Happy Attitudes.

M	O	D	G	N	I	K	P	B	P
E	H	L	R	O	O	P	E	A	H
D	B	U	E	L	D	A	A	S	A
P	E	M	G	M	T	S	C	E	P
A	Y	T	N	E	S	T	E	D	P
H	U	P	U	R	E	H	M	U	Y
E	G	O	H	C	K	I	A	T	P
A	O	I	G	I	E	R	K	I	P
V	G	K	N	F	U	S	E	T	Y
E	L	B	M	U	H	T	R	A	O
N	A	K	E	L	R	T	S	E	E
T	H	I	R	T	Y	E	N	B	P

This is how you should pray:

Find this in Matthew 6:9-13

Don't worry about:

school work

illness

dogs

clothes

food

money

weather

Look up Matthew 6:24-34

God looks after these:

He will look after you.

Draw a picture of yourself:

Use the code to find out what this verse says:

D	N	O	T
W	R	Y	A
B	U	M	H

Matthew 6:34

Find this story in Matthew 7: 24-27

Wise man

digs foundations

built on R _ _ _

hears and obeys Jesus.

Foolish man

no foundations

built on S _ _ _ hears,

but doesn't obey Jesus.

Tick those things which could be 'storms' in life:

illness

argument

winning a race

birthday parties

losing a pet

Word search

D	E	W	O	L	F	R	E	V	O
E	L	O	C	F	V	K	C	O	R
R	A	D	K	O	A	B	E	I	Y
U	C	O	T	O	N	L	V	L	E
O	K	W	L	L	C	E	L	A	D
P	O	N	I	I	R	W	D	S	R
T	H	O	U	S	E	A	I	A	E
S	R	A	B	H	E	R	I	N	E
Y	R	I	V	E	N	S	A	N	D
O	B	U	L	T	Y	L	T	E	S

BUILT   OBEY
DOWN   POURED
FALL   ROCK
FOOLISH   SAND
HOUSE   WIND
                WISE

Unscramble the names of these people who help build houses:

1. REPENTCAR   _____

2. RELICKABRY   _____

3. REBLUMP   _____

4. RETAPIN   _____

A Man sowed good seed.

The enemy came and sowed some weeds.

Everyone was asleep.

The servants asked if they should pull up the weeds.

At harvest time the wheat and weeds were gathered together and the weeds were burnt.

The man told them to wait until harvest time.

Can you fit the words in?

8 LETTERS
SLEEPING

7 LETTERS
HARVEST
PARABLE

6 LETTERS
BURNED

5 LETTERS
ENEMY
FIELD
SOWED
WEEDS
WHEAT

4 LETTERS
GROW
ROOT

Find this story in Matthew 13

Find this story in Matthew 13

The kingdom of heaven is like treasure hidden in a field.

Matthew 13:44

Which path leads to the treasure?

Word search

BEADS   BROOCH
BRACELET   DIAMONDS

CHAIN
CHEST
COINS
CROWN
CUP
GEM
GOLD
JEWELS
MONEY
NECKLACE
PEARLS
RINGS
RUBY
SILVER
TREASURE

N	S	E	B	E	A	D	S	E	G
I	T	D	O	Y	M	E	G	G	C
A	A	R	N	M	B	O	N	O	S
H	I	H	E	O	O	U	I	L	I
C	K	C	C	A	M	N	R	D	L
O	U	D	K	H	S	A	E	B	V
O	S	P	L	D	E	U	I	Y	E
R	I	V	A	P	A	S	R	D	R
B	R	A	C	E	L	E	T	E	W
I	S	L	E	W	E	J	B	T	N
R	E	N	C	R	O	W	N	S	E

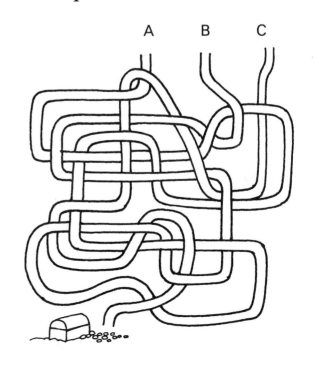

Read this story in Matthew 17 or Mark 9.

This is my own dear Son — listen to him!

Mark 9:7

Word search

CLOUD   MOSES
ELIJAH   MOUNTAIN
JAMES   PETER
JESUS   TENTS
JOHN   WHITER

P	S	M	O	N	S	T	N	S
E	E	T	O	U	W	I	J	C
P	M	L	S	H	A	N	A	L
E	A	E	I	T	N	S	M	O
T	J	T	N	J	E	S	S	U
E	E	U	H	S	A	N	H	D
R	O	S	O	H	W	H	T	O
M	E	M	J	L	C	N	E	S

Put the first letter of the picture in the box:

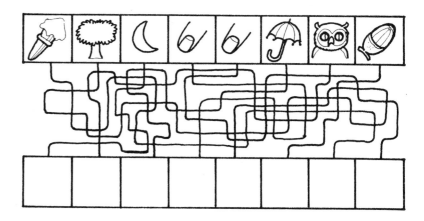

Read this story in Matthew 18:21-35

Forgive others.

Word search

M	I	L	L	O	S	N	S	C	F
I	S	A	P	C	H	I	L	O	D
A	S	N	E	O	D	E	R	E	C
J	N	E	U	E	U	G	B	N	H
A	O	G	R	O	A	N	G	R	I
L	I	G	R	V	P	O	D	G	L
I	L	N	E	Y	A	E	K	S	D
S	L	I	A	J	B	N	F	O	R
E	I	K	V	T	K	I	T	G	E
F	M	S	E	V	E	N	T	Y	N

ANGRY   JAIL   SERVANT
CHILDREN   KING   SEVENTY
DEBT   MILLIONS
FORGAVE   POUNDS

Make 10 or more words out of the word FORGIVENESS

Which one says sorry?

Find this story in
Matthew 20

Word search

H	G	B	A	B	C	E	D	Q	G	T	S	A	L
F	I	R	S	T	G	A	E	H	B	A	M	N	A
B	R	C	F	A	P	O	O	C	D	O	P	N	N
D	E	N	V	I	O	U	S	W	L	L	L	D	D
A	D	M	O	C	R	C	N	F	C	O			O
Y	X	O	E	S	R	E	K	R	O	W			
Z	N	H	E	M	H	I	J	D	N				
A	E	C	H	K	P	W	R	F	E				
	Y	A	P	L	A	A	E	G	R				
	O	N	M	G	Y	D	R	L	L				
	P	Q	E	E	C	R	A	Z	D				
	R	S	N	L	F	S	C	Y	F				
	S	I	B	T	B	T	M	M	E				
	V	T	D	X	Y	M	H	K	J				
	A	E	U	I	W	D	U	L	W				
	T	I	V	I	V	M	R	V					
	S	U	O	R	E	N	E	G					

ENVIOUS   LAST
FIRST   MEN
GENEROUS   MONEY
GRUMBLE   PAY
HIRED   WORKERS
HOUR   WAGES
LANDOWNER

The first shall be last and the last shall be first.

Matthew 20:16

Which way to the Vineyard?

Don't be envious of other people.

Find this story in Matthew 22:1-14

You are invited
to
A WEDDING FEAST
Barbecued Oxen
and Calves
Wear Correct Dress

Write the name of
these objects in the boxes:

Many are invited but few are chosen. Matthew 22:14

Find this story in Matthew 25

£5000 became £10000

use it
or

£2000 became £

lose
it

£1000 became

However small you are, or useless you feel, you can always be useful for God.

Word search

D	O	D	N	T	B	E	L	A	Z	Y
M	O	N	E	Y	B	U	T	S	Y	L
C	O	A	P	E	Y	T	E	H	U	S
D	Y	S	A	L	D	R	V	F	S	I
N	G	U	T	B	V	C	H	L	E	A
U	R	O	D	A	I	T	C	T	L	Y
O	P	H	N	R	I	L	O	D	E	B
R	E	T	S	A	M	H	I	D	S	I
G	S	H	F	P	A	D	N	T	S	T
L	A	P	L	A	B	A	S	E	Y	L

ABILITY
COINS
FAITHFUL
GROUND
HID
LAZY
MASTER
MONEY
PARABLE
SERVANTS
THOUSAND
USELESS

Help the lazy servant find his money:

Mary has chosen the right thing. Luke 10:42

Word search

There are 26 girls' names hidden here, 10 across and 16 down, all beginning with 'M'. How many can you find?

M	A	T	I	L	D	A	M	M	M	M	M	M
M	M	M	M	M	M	M	I	R	I	A	M	M
M	A	R	I	E	M	I	R	M	M	D	E	M
M	B	M	M	L	M	C	A	A	A	E	L	M
M	L	M	M	A	M	H	N	G	R	L	I	M
M	E	G	A	N	I	E	D	G	C	I	S	A
M	M	M	R	I	L	L	A	I	I	N	S	R
M	M	M	Y	E	D	L	M	E	A	E	A	T
M	A	R	G	A	R	E	T	M	M	M	M	H
A	M	M	M	M	E	M	M	T	A	Y	M	A
D	U	A	M	M	D	M	A	U	R	E	E	N
G	R	V	M	M	M	A	M	M	I	M	M	M
E	I	I	M	M	M	N	M	M	O	L	L	Y
M	E	S	M	A	U	D	M	O	N	I	C	A
M	L	M	M	M	M	Y	M	M	M	M	M	M

Put the first letter of the picture in each box to find the name of Mary and Martha's village:

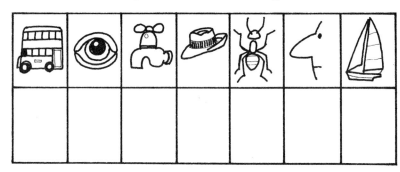

Find Mary and Martha's house.

Find this story in Luke 12

Where your treasure is that's where your heart is.

Luke 12:34

Word search

P	A	R	A	B	L	E	W	P	H	P	O	T	H	O	U	G	H	T	B	U	L	D	E	S	T	R	D
R	L	E	O	L	A	A	O	S	U	A	A	H	E	D	E	S	T	R	I	R	E	T	S	T	A	E	E
I	L	A	E	L	I	S	T	O	E	R	I	C	H	E	S	T	O	R	G	S	A	K	R	C	S	W	M
C	E	G	C	S	T	B	R	T	M	A	S	O	F	L	E	S	Y	M	G	O	A	E	A	T	T	A	A
L	E	R	D	E	U	E	A	S	Y	L	G	E	G	E	P	H	E	R	A	T	A	G	R	W	O	R	N
E	F	E	B	I	G	G	E	R	S	B	I	P	S	R	E	R	E	M	E	S	F	O	O	L	E	E	D
S	M	A	L	G	S	I	H	G	N	E	P	H	P	A	R	E	S	E	U	M	Y	O	S	E	L	H	E
A	Y	D	P	O	S	E	R	O	T	S	I	H	T	Y	D	P	O	R	Y	N	W	D	N	H	S	C	D
N	S	P	E	O	S	P	O	O	S	S	E	S	S	I	O	F	E	I	H	T	A	K	T	R	A	T	E
T	A	K	E	E	T	I	O	L	G	H	U	O	H	T	R	A	E	S	U	R	E	S	N	U	E	A	L
W	E	A	R	T	H	O	U	H	T	G	S	E	O	S	N	O	I	S	S	E	S	S	O	P	O	W	E

BARNS
BIGGER
BUILD
DEMANDED
DESTROY
EASY
EAT
FOOL
GOOD
GREED
HEART
MERRY
MYSELF
PARABLE
PLACE
POSSESSIONS
PURSES
RICHES
STORES
TAKE
THIEF
THOUGHT
TREASURE
WATCH
WEAR

> **Jesus says we should not store up treasures on earth, where the moth can destroy and the thief can steal things away, but store up for yourself treasures in heaven.**

Put a tick by the treasures you would rather have:

A new cassette recorder

love

a new skateboard

joy

sweets

kindness

patience

money

Find this story in John 4

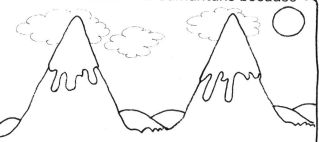

The Jews hated the Samaritans because

they argued about which mountain they should worship God on. The Samaritans thought one, the Jews thought another.

A long time ago Jews had married people who were not Jews and their children were the Samaritans. They had mixed blood.

Life-giving water.

John 4:10

Word search

A	M	S	A	R	I	C	K	E	T	B
A	S	N	A	M	O	W	E	T	U	U
E	T	J	I	M	O	U	A	C	P	C
P	E	T	E	A	A	P	K	T	E	J
I	K	H	I	R	T	R	L	L	E	W
H	C	I	A	R	U	N	I	S	D	R
S	U	R	H	I	P	S	U	T	B	D
R	B	S	J	E	S	S	A	O	A	I
O	O	T	B	D	U	S	E	L	M	N
W	U	Y	L	A	N	R	E	T	E	K
E	S	D	R	I	N	K	P	M	N	M
O	U	N	S	H	I	D	A	N	I	E

BUCKET   THIRSTY

DEEP   WATER

DRINK   WELL

ETERNAL   WOMAN

HUSBAND   WORSHIP

JERUSALEM

JESUS

MARRIED

MESSIAH

MOUNTAIN

SAMARITAN

Which way to the well?

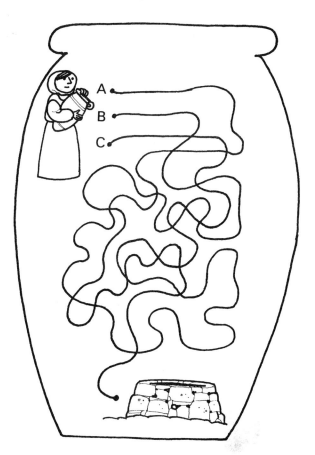

Put the first letter of the picture in each box:

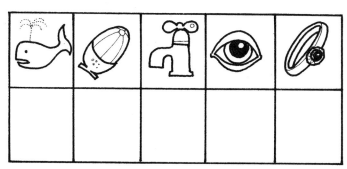

This Story comes from John 20

Blessed are those who have not seen and yet have believed. John 20:29

Break this code and find out what we should do when we doubt:

7	3	1	6		2	1	10	11	3	5	4	12	

8	4	2		11	13	9	5	13	14	13

O	D	T	N	I	P	S	A	L	U	B	G	E	V
1	2	3	4	5	6	7	8	9	10	11	12	13	14

Word search

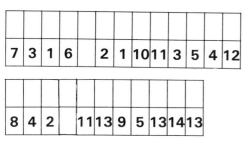

BELIEVED
DOOR
DOUBT
HAND
JESUS
LOCKED
NAILS
SIDE
THOMAS

I don't think God can heal her.

I don't think God hears me when I pray.

I don't think anyone loves me.

Put a tick by the doubts you have had.

I don't think she will become a Christian.

I don't think God can keep me safe.

Find this story in Acts 8:26-40

Philip baptised him.

Acts 8:38

Fit the words in the boxes:

3 LETTERS
RAN

4 LETTERS
HOME
ROAD

5 LETTERS
WATER

8 LETTERS
BAPTISER

6 LETTERS
DESERT
ISAIAH
PHILIP
SPIRIT

7 LETTERS
CHARIOT

9 LETTERS
ETHIOPIAN
JERUSALEM

JERUSALEM

Which road goes past the water?

GAZA

Think about good things.

Philippians 4:8

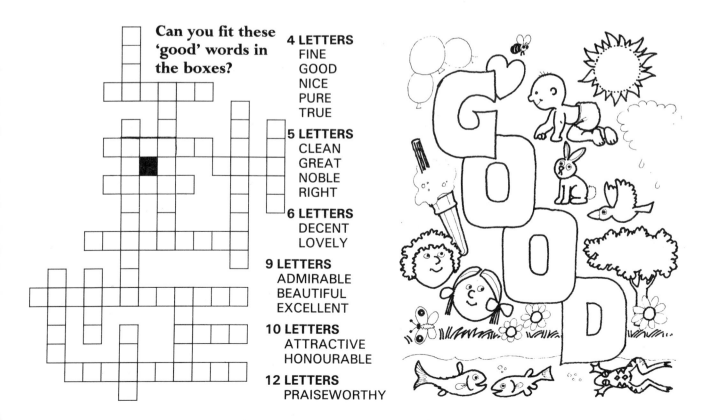

Can you fit these 'good' words in the boxes?

4 LETTERS
FINE
GOOD
NICE
PURE
TRUE

5 LETTERS
CLEAN
GREAT
NOBLE
RIGHT

6 LETTERS
DECENT
LOVELY

9 LETTERS
ADMIRABLE
BEAUTIFUL
EXCELLENT

10 LETTERS
ATTRACTIVE
HONOURABLE

12 LETTERS
PRAISEWORTHY

Find the book of Philemon. 'Onesimus' means 'useful'.

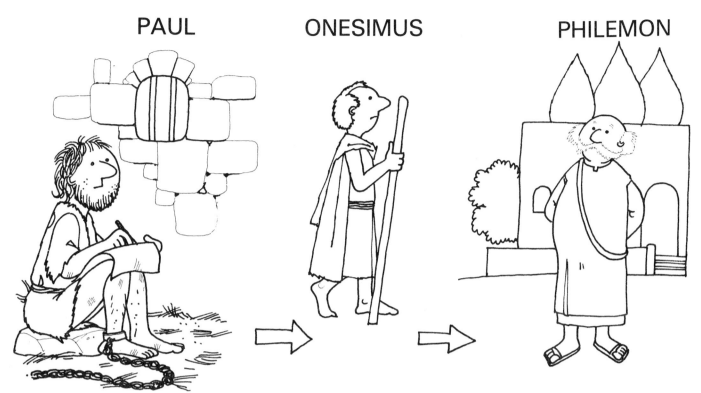

PAUL   ONESIMUS   PHILEMON

Forgive as the Lord forgave you.

Colossians 3:13

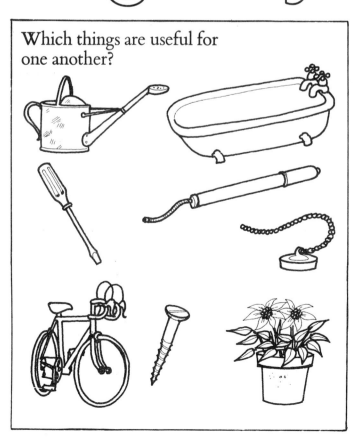

Which things are useful for one another?

Word search

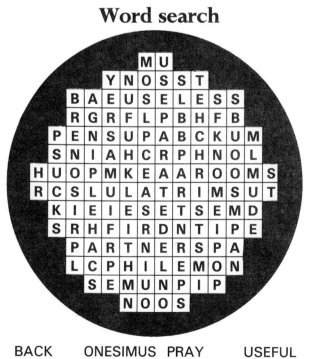

MU							

```
        M U
      Y N O S S T
    B A E U S E L E S S
    R G R F L P B H F B
  P E N S U P A B C K U M
  S N I A H C R P H N O L
  H U O P M K E A A R O O M S
  R C S L U L A T R I M S U T
  K I E I E S E T S E M D
  S R H F I R D N T I P E
    P A R T N E R S P A
    L C P H I L E M O N
      S E M U N P I P
        N O O S
```

BACK   ONESIMUS   PRAY   USEFUL
CHAINS   PARTNER   PRISONER   USELESS
CHRIST   PAUL   ROOM
HELPING   PHILEMON   SEPARATED

Find this in James 3

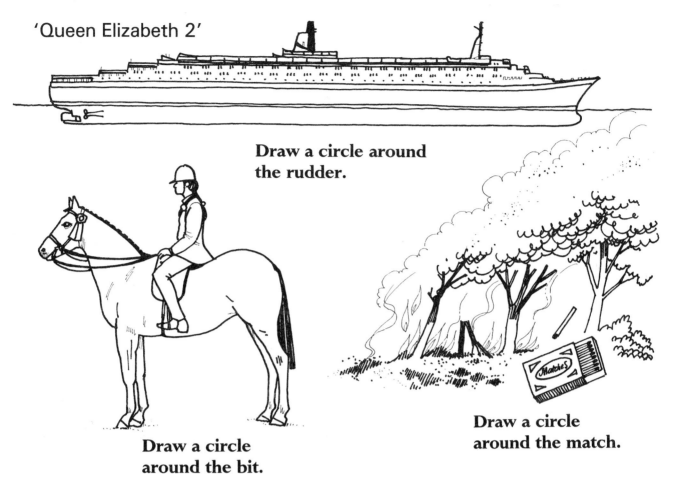

'Queen Elizabeth 2'

Draw a circle around the rudder.

Draw a circle around the bit.

Draw a circle around the match.

The mouth speaks what the heart is full of. Luke 6:45

THE MOUTH TEST

Before you speak take the Mouth Test.

1. Is it true?

2. Is it helpful?

3. Is it loving?

Word search

BIT	SHIP
CONTROL	STEERED
ENCOURAGE	TAME
FIRE	THANKS
FLAME	TONGUE
FOREST	WORDS
HORSE	
MOUTH	
RUDDER	

F	O	R	S	E	T	B	F	L
L	I	E	I	S	I	E	O	E
E	R	R	H	T	M	R	R	L
M	N	I	P	O	T	I	E	S
E	P	C	U	N	R	F	S	T
W	S	T	O	G	E	S	T	E
O	H	C	G	U	E	M	E	M
R	U	D	D	E	R	I	A	U
D	N	O	S	K	N	A	H	T
S	T	E	E	R	E	D	G	P
T	O	G	U	F	L	A	M	E

What can you say to encourage someone today?